I'm Not Successful Because I Don't Want To Be

A Hard Look
In The Mirror
&
A Reality Check
For Your Life

Suzan M. Stroud

I'm Not Successful Because I Don't Want To Be
Copyright © 2010 by Suzan M. Stroud

ISBN-13: 978-14538-8404-1
ISBN-10: 1453884041

All rights reserved. No part of this book may be reproduced or transmitted in any form or by any means without written permission from the author.

Published in the United States of America

Cover Design By: Angette Williams & The Fancy Graphics

All Scripture quotations, unless otherwise indicated are taken from the Holy Bible, New King James Version

Dedication

I dedicate this book to my loving parents Leroy & Esther Pearson, who were instrumental in helping me to understand the fundamentals of life and success. They raised me to be the confident woman, wife, mother and friend that I am today. I especially thank my dad for the countless hours we spent in the bookstore on most weekends and my mom for all of the extra homework assignments and the time she spent preparing me for greatness; it has all attributed to fulfilling my purpose in life.

I also dedicate this to Regina Harris and Richard Austin for their love and prayers over the years. God nurtured and kept me just as you had asked Him to and I thank you for being who you are and welcoming me into your lives and your families.

Table of Contents

Introduction………………………………………….4

Take A Look, What Do You See?………..8

Coulda, Woulda, Shoulda……………...14

Why Have Success and I Not Met?……..22

Vision……………………………………...28

Passion………………………………….. 40

Motivation ……………………………….50

Education……………………………......60

Funding ………………………………….72

Taking Action …………………………..78

Conclusion ……………………………..88

Success Summary Outline……………..92

******

Letter to Reader

Recommended Resources

Acknowledgment

To my husband John, your endless example of dedication, sacrifice, sleepless nights and your courage to step out on faith is one of the main reasons I've been able to complete this project. You motivated me in a way that only a loving husband could; and I'm glad I finally took the time to sit still and walk out just a small facet of my purpose here on this earth. I love you with all of my heart.

And to my children, Artee' and John, I love you both dearly. You're the reason that I keep pressing through and I look forward to witnessing your future success.

I want to thank my friends and family for their labor of love and contribution in assuring that this book would be the success it is destined to be.

Introduction

The opinions, statements and ideas mentioned in this book are solely from or about the author. If there is any similarity to the readers, their family, friends and/or co-workers it is purely coincidental and hence is the reason for the writing of this book. I have written this book for "**You**" the future entrepreneur, athlete, actor/actress, musician, singer, educator, journalist, model, healthcare professional, attorney, astronaut, etc. The six characteristics discussed in this book are applicable for all areas of your life; you just have to choose to make them work for you.

If you're anything like me, over the course of your life you have excelled in all (if not most) of your places of employment; you've spent time assisting others in their quest for success; shared a few great ideas with them and even harbored some of those ideas for yourself. But as I reflect over the years and think of all the mystic inventions and bright ideas I've come up with, some I've worked on and others I just allowed to sit idle and even die. I realized that I had allowed something in my life (family, career or school) to convince me to put all those dreams and ideas on the backburner never to see or think about them ever again. I never considered that I would pay the price later down the line and once that time had passed it would be gone forever. For some reason, I always thought that I would have more time to get it done.

So, if you delight in wasting valuable time, having no vision for your life or you enjoy slaving away for someone else 2,080 hours a year working a job that you totally dread – then this book is **ABSOLUTELY NOT** for you. However, if you're ready for "A hard look in the mirror and a reality check for your life" then you are hereby permitted to proceed reading the following chapters. My intent as you read through the following pages is to cause you to be so frustrated with your life that you'll get rid of that lackadaisical way of thinking, destroy any fear that you have about moving forward, re-build your confidence and self-esteem or just awaken you to **DO SOMETHING** productive, fulfilling and significant with your life. You know what it is, it's that *"something"* that drives you to get out of bed every day, it kicks in an immeasurable level of excitement and at the end of the day it leaves you feeling as though your pursuit has been accomplished. I don't know what your *"something"* is, but you sure do.

I've taken the liberty of writing a book which illustrates why it took me so long to reach my desired level of success. Hopefully, my transparency will position you to get there a lot sooner and as we journey through the book together it will serve as a compass guiding you towards your desired level of success. This compass that you currently hold in your hand is the practical tool you'll need to begin your journey to success. It is very important that we keep our compass pointing in the direction of Success. You will not just read this book, but at the end of each chapter, you will find Focal Points and Success Strategies that will serve as a catalyst to get you in gear and on track. I encourage you to ponder the Focal Points and answer all of the Success Strategy questions. Then at the end of the book you will be asked to complete the Success Summary Outline which is a culmination of the entire book causing you to hopefully draw closer your dreams.

Focal Points – Highlights of the chapter that should be used to assist you with recapping important points within the chapter.

Success Strategy – Here is where you will indicate your ideal strategy as it relates to that chapter.

Success Summary Outline – At the conclusion of this book you will be given the opportunity to create an outline describing how you plan to activate the six characteristics discussed in the book and how you will go about activating your personal success journey. This outline will serve as your map to get you started and hopefully keep you motivated. You must commit to reviewing and meditating on the Focal Points and answering the Success Strategy questions. If you are unable to commit to doing any of the above, then **PUT THIS BOOK DOWN!**

Take A Look, What Do You See?

Before we take another step and go any further, I want you to get up right now from where you are and go stand in front of a mirror. It doesn't matter if it's the compact mirror in your purse or the mirror in your bathroom; I just want you to be able to see yourself. I already know what you're thinking, *"I'm not going to stand in front of a mirror....please!"* *"That's Silly!"* Well, ok if that's the case, shut the book now give it away and don't waste another minute of your time. But, if you think more of yourself and want more out of life, then hurry up and get to that mirror. Are you there yet? Great! Now I want you to take a long hard look at yourself and tell me what you see? You need to make strong eye contact with yourself and really check yourself out. I know you're looking good and you can't take your eyes off of yourself, but when you look into that mirror beyond the make-up, hair style and contact lenses, what do you *"really"* see? Do you see a success or a failure? Do you see potential or progress? Do you see a person of strength or one of weakness? Do you see a person who can change the world and make a difference? Do you see someone who is happy or depressed? Do you see greatness? Do you see an individual of great value and wealth? Do you see a person who has a strong self-image and high regard for themselves? Finally, do you see a successful individual with the ability to gain and produce wealth? I sure hope so, because if you don't see it then you can't become it.

Did you know that what you think about yourself can be the determining factor on how successful you will be? I don't know what your responses to the preceding questions were, but what I do know is whatever you see; only you can control the perspective and the outcome. My "mirror" experience came to me one morning while sitting in my home office (unemployed) looking out the window only 2 weeks after my 40th birthday. As I sat there feeling depressed, hopeless and with no grip on the direction of my life, I asked myself, "what had I done with my life and why was I not where I thought I should have been at that time?" And I literally heard the still voice within respond immediately, "because you didn't want to be." That brief conversation I had with myself was the instant inspiration for writing this book, because in that instance I realized how I had allowed myself to cozy up with defeat and I hadn't even noticed its deplorable scent. I was so angry with myself, but soon realized getting angry was futile if I wasn't planning to do anything about it. I was also feeling a little guilty for thinking I had so much time when I was in my teens and twenties to figure out what I wanted to do with my life, that I just allowed time to slip away. When I took that hard look in the mirror, I saw a person who, if given a task or project could really move and make things happen-but beneath the façade of being "Ms. Wonderful" and "Ms. Dependable" I was a slacker in my own destiny. YES I SAID IT! I called myself a slacker, but not in the sense of being lazy or not wanting to do anything, but a person who somehow subtly befriended procrastination. I can honestly admit to you that I take personal responsibility for my lack of success, but what I will not do is; sit around and feel sorry for myself and blame others. I had to wake up, get up and then do something about it. And so do you! You must make a conscious decision from this day forward that you will make a concerted effort to believe in who God created you to be and not take lightly what He created you to do. Genesis 1:26 says; **"Then God said, "Let us make man in Our image, according to Our likeness; let them have dominion over the fish of the sea, over the birds of the air, and over the cattle, over all the earth and over every creeping thing that creeps on the earth"(NKJV.)** You've got to realize that whatever is getting you down or holding you back only has that power because you relinquished it. It gained its strength and momentum because you decided to take a passive role in your own life. At some point in my life I became complacent and just allowed life to happen instead of taking control and making life happen. Now is the time for you to take back your power and walk in your God given authority to rule what's been ruling you, take back what belongs to you and open your arms to embrace your newest associate: **SUCCESS.**

If you're feeling like your life is going nowhere and that good things only happen to other people or you're not smart enough to be greater than what you are right now – then you're probably right. As long as you have that negative perspective that's exactly the way things are always going to be; but today is a new day and you've _just_ agreed to transform your thinking. If you're going to be successful at anything (weight loss, business, sports, music, etc.) you will have to want it more than anything else and be willing to overcome the obstacles that will greet you on your way there.

You have nothing to fear; be strong and courageous because everything you'll need for your life journey is already within you. Just like the mustard seed, though it's very small in size, it has everything it needs to grow and become a large leafy green. In order to locate what's within you it will require increased patience and an in depth search of your inner being. There's hidden wisdom and knowledge within; you just have to take the necessary time to discover it. There is something about you that I think you should know and that is, you are <u>very</u> convincing. You ask how I could make such a keen observation about someone whom I barely know. Well, I figure that if you are not where you should be in life it is probably because <u>YOU</u> have convinced <u>YOU</u> that you're not smart enough, rich enough, or you don't have the looks and what it takes to be in business for yourself. I bet you can count on all fingers and toes the number of times you've had this conversation with yourself.

Now, go back to that same mirror and take another look, except this time I don't want you to tell me what you see-just **BECOME IT!**

Focal Points for Take A Look, What Do You See?

- ➢ Believe that you have been provided with what it takes to succeed.
- ➢ Think and speak only things that are positive.
- ➢ Only you can change the perspective that you have about yourself.
- ➢ Take dominion and rule over what's been ruling you.

Success Strategy:

1. Write a positive quote about the new perspective you have about yourself and make it a ritual to repeat it every day.

_____
_____
_____
_____
_____

2. Complete the following statement; I will take dominion and rule over;

_____
_____
_____
_____

Coulda, Woulda, Shoulda

  Coulda, Woulda, and Shoulda are what I refer to as the three stooges of mental agony and defeat. How many times have you tortured yourself by constantly saying "I coulda been a teacher if I had gone to college," I woulda been a professional athlete if the coach had not cut me from the team," "I shoulda taken that job five years ago, I'd probably be making more money by now."   I call this mental agony and defeat because for the longest time I lived with this thought process. I would constantly remind myself almost every day about my coulda's, woulda's and shoulda's. And after harping on them for a long period to time and like termites, the agony of failure started to slowly eat away my desire to try. There's a host of coulda's, woulda's and shoulda's that you can taunt yourself with, but why waste valuable mental energy on past opportunities that you don't have the ability to do anything about. I should know, because I taunted myself for years about my decision not to attend college. I don't regret it to the degree where I did not think that I was smart; I regretted not having the full college experience which I believe hindered my full earning potential because I didn't have a college degree.   Since I was long past the age of entering into college I had to remind myself that it was the past and since there was nothing that I could do about what was already behind me that I needed to let it go. And so I did! Have you ever experienced this? Maybe your story is not exactly like mine, but I know we've both shared a dip in the coulda, woulda, shoulda pool. Anytime you feel your thoughts digressing back to your past failures or missed opportunities, do as I've learned to do; immediately change those thoughts and focus on what you can do "right now" and then take action. I call these moments "past-op" visits as opposed to a "post-op" visit. Whenever you have any type of a surgical procedure the surgeon typically schedules a post-op visit which allows him to go back to make sure the area of incision is healing properly and bacteria and infection are not forming in the wound. We do just the opposite with a "past-op" visit, instead of working towards healing our wounds and letting go of our missed opportunities, we infect ourselves with negative talk, doubt and thoughts of defeat never giving ourselves the opportunity to heal mentally. Learn to let your past and missed opportunities be just that, your past opportunities. Awaken and walk into the new opportunities that await you. You'll be surprised at the mysteries within that have been waiting to be unleashed.

As long as you continue to grasp and gnaw at the things of the past you'll never be able to get a good grip on your future. Ask yourself this question, are my Coulda's, Woulda's and Shoulda's my own personal regrets, desires and aspirations or are they what someone else thought I should have become? Who am I trying to make happy? If what you are doing is merely for the sake of someone else then I hate to be the one to tell you that you will always be faced with Coulda's, Woulda's and Shoulda's, because your life will be based on satisfying their desire for your life instead of what God desires for you to be.

I remember this dance we use to do when I was in grade school called the Hokey Pokey. It went something like this; *"you put your right leg out, you put your right leg in, you put your right leg in and you shake it all about-you do the hokey pokey then you turn yourself around, that's what it's all about."* Hokey Pokey! First of all, what exactly is the hokey pokey and really, what is it all about. I'll tell you, it's about one's inability to make up their mind and make a final decision. If you sing the song long enough and reflect on your decision making process, you'll see that I am right. Keep a keen ear and a sharp eye out for those cute, likeable and simple things in life that attempt to enter into your mindset. It's not the huge obvious distractions that will get you off track, it's those that appear subtle and harmless that will wreck your destiny.

You should have come to the place by now where you recognize the "who or what" in your life that has the strongest influence over you. Is it a negative or positive influence? Is it pushing you toward or away from your purpose and destiny? Does it leave you feeling drained or energized? I'll share 3 possible reasons on how we arrive at the Coulda, Woulda and Shoulda stage;

You've talked yourself out of moving forward.
- You experience ping pong thoughts of "I know I can" or "no I can't." Your wavering decisions keep you standing still.

There's fear of failing or succeeding.
- Thoughts of failure override any possibility of taking action, so there is no way that success can prevail.

You attempt to please others.
- Dependence on the approval or acceptance of others will diminish your dreams and leave you with feeling empty and hopeless.

Now that you know how you've arrived at this very dark place, what are you going to do about it?

The Future of Your Success

Your future and your success is just that-**YOURS**. If there are any regrets in your midst about where you are in life, it's a regret that you bear all on your own. If you are not where you thought you should be or doing the one thing you enjoy so much that you would do it for free then you're allowing your "passion passport" to slowly drift away (We'll discuss more about that in the next chapter).

Imagine you're in a row boat out in the middle of the ocean, when suddenly you lose one of your oars. This very thing happened to me one year at summer camp; and since I am not a swimmer, my initial reaction was one of fear and panic. But the longer I sat there the further my oar drifted away from the boat and out of my reach. These oars are used as a metaphoric representation of you reaching your destiny, so are you just going to sit there and continue to watch as it just drifts away? Well that's exactly what you're doing when you allow your passion to get away from you. If you don't pick up and reignite your passion, it will continue to drift away and soon it will no longer be within your sight. When this happens you start thinking about it being so far out of your reach that you won't even bother going after it. Success does not come easy and will not always be within your immediate reach, sometimes it will require stretching-mentally and physically.
Success is about a written plan and if you have no plan your future is going to be filled with haphazard decision making and sadly, full of disappointments.

If you've ever mentally planned out your entire day or week in advance you will know that in the beginning you're feeling charged and filled with good intentions of getting it all done, but for some reason or another you never seem to get any of it done. Why is that? I'll tell you why; you didn't write it down. It was a thought that became a vapor instead of a visible goal. There are countless distractions that you could encounter in any given day, and therefore, you should start each day with a plan-and stick to it.

Starting right now, make an intentional effort to change any negative emotions or lackadaisical thinking that causes you to remain stuck in the "going nowhere pit." This kind of thinking will zap your energy – so naturally you NEVER feel like doing anything beyond your normal work day. Does your day to day after work routine consists of going home, sitting on the sofa, channel surfing, takeout dinner, more channel surfing or TiVo and then off to bed. I know for awhile mine did. But I had to learn the hard way that you won't get where you're trying to go by doing that every day. From now on your new routine consists of changing your vocabulary to begin using words such as, I shall, I must and I will. From now on when you get home from work avoid sitting on the sofa watching television the first hour that you're home and instead begin seeking wisdom and direction from God by meditating for at least 15 minutes. Watch and see how your mental energy begins to explode and your drive to produce increases. I'm beginning to see those wheels turning; your heart is racing and you're getting "that take charge of my life and destiny attitude." I guarantee that if you get excited about your life a whole new world of creative ideas and energy will begin to overwhelm you.

So there, now that we've gotten that settled, we won't waste anymore time talking about this and you agree that you will no longer ponder thoughts of what may have been and focus your attention on what you are yet to become. Remember, your future successes will always be greater than your past failures.

Focal Points for Coulda, Woulda, and Shoulda:

- Let it Go!
- No more regrets! Think Positive!
- Look toward the future and move forward.
- No more "past-op" visits.
- I shall, I must, I will.

Success Strategy:

List any past regrets you need to let go of so that you will be able to move forward with your plan:

1. _____
2. _____
3. _____
4. _____
5. _____

Additional Comments:

Why Have Success And I Not Met?

In the previous chapter I mentioned the importance of making a list of your goals visible. How can you begin to achieve what you cannot see? If you currently do not have your own formula for success, then we will use this one until you create one of your own.

Goals + Vision = Achievement

Simply put, the outcome is achievement. Which brings me to our next point-if you cannot see your vision how will you recognize your personal success? What is your definition of success? What does it look like? Is it acquiring great wealth and fame, an executive level position with a corner office or maybe it's where you live or what you drive? However you define it, be sure that you are not allowing the expectations of your family, friends or even society to determine what success means for you. If you were to personally meet Oprah Winfrey, Michael Jordon or even President Obama, there would be no doubt in your mind that you've met these very well known individuals. Why, because you can measure their success by what you can see and what they've actually accomplished. What will be the measure of your success, would you be able to recognize it? You could be successful right now and not even know it.

It is important to know that God's definition of success is entirely different than ours, so be sure that you are seeking wisdom, guidance and direction from Him. One of His many definitions for success is to be obedient and in direct alignment with His will, desire and calling for your life-whatever that may be. In Matthew 6:33 it reads "**But seek first the kingdom of God and all these things shall be added to you (NKJV).**" What that means is; everything that you ever desire to obtain, to be or get to is wrapped up in your "seeking Him." If you make Him priority and a primal focus in your life, those things that seemed impossible will begin to manifest. I must have read this particular passage of scripture a dozen times, but it was not until I "really" read it by slowly reading only 4 words at a time; that I really came to understand what it was saying to me. Now why would God write such a thing if He did not want you to have all that He has in store for you? God desires success to come from your life more than you do. Your desire should be in alignment with Him and as the verse just stated "all these things *shall* be added to you."

Passion or Procrastination

If you've ever had the opportunity to travel outside of the United States, you know that international travel requires you to carry a U.S. Passport if you plan to enter into another country. A passport is your key to international travel. It allows you to experience a variety of culture, food, art and music; it literally exposes you to an entirely different world. The same holds true with your "*passion passport*", when in the driver's seat of your success it will take you to destinations unknown. You will face being detained for an indefinite amount of time if you to attempt to travel into the world of success without any passion. In order to meet up with the people of South Africa, New Zealand or China you will need a U.S. Passport and if you're going to meet up with success to further explore your destiny, you must have your "passion passport" activated and with you at all times. However, if you find that you are lacking in passion then you're probably loaded down with the other "p" that will affect your success and that would be **PROCRASTINATION**.

Procrastination means that we intentionally and habitually put things off. This word is an exact description of why I had been delayed in meeting the abundant success that God had desired and why I am not in the secure financial position that I should be in by now. It seems to follow me everywhere I go and it gets into everything that I attempt to do. I have yet to find a foolproof way of overcoming procrastination, but I did find a way to keep me from totally being submissive to it. I came up with an acronym that I would use to overtake my procrastination when it came along. I refer to it as TAP, **Think, Act and Produce**. Meaning when you think on something you must immediately act on it and from that action you will produce. Thinking is easy, in fact you can sit around all day long and think of all kinds of ideas and scenarios, but the rest of the world and the people that need your vision to come to pass cannot get to their next level in life and neither will you. In order to put legs to your plan it is going to require action and action requires mental as well as physical energy. So what are you going to do, are you just going to sit there like a lump on a log feeling sorry for yourself and continue to think that success is for other people and not you. Or are you going to bring this thing to life.

However, before you can successfully manage your procrastination you must identify why you do it. There are many factors that could contribute to why we haven't achieved our desired level of success and why procrastination always gets the victory.

Listed below you will find a few of those factors that I had allowed to hold me back;

- **Vision**
- **Passion**
- **Motivation**
- **Education**
- **Funding**
- **Taking Action**

You may have your own list of hindrances and you can feel free to add them to the list, but for now let's discuss each one of these individually.

Focal Points for Why Have Success And I Not Met?
- Remember our success formula:
    Goals + Vision = Achievement
- Assure that your definition of success is in alignment with God's definition.
- Passion or Procrastination – which do you hold fast to?
- TAP – Think, Act and Produce

Success Strategy:

Briefly Describe Your Idea of Success:

_____

_____

_____

_____

_____

_____

_____

VISION

HOW YOU SEE IT!

Vision

"The only thing worse than being blind is having sight and no vision"

Helen Keller

You've probably known since you were in grade school what you "thought" you wanted to do with your life. When I was younger, it was really easy to see what I wanted to be, because I was exposed to role models in every arena of my life. I remember when I was a little girl I thought I wanted to become a teacher but that was short lived. Then somewhere in my thirties I had this bright idea to become a firefighter. Wow! What extremes! But nonetheless, I had these particular careers (and many others) in sight, but I was missing the vision that connected sight with manifestation. In Habakkuk 2:2 it reads; "**Write the vision and make it plain on tablets, that he may run who reads it (NKJV).**" A critical aspect needed to your vision is that at some point you have to write it down. Habakkuk clearly instructs that. How can you run with it, if it is not written down? Well, in order to get to that point, you will need to shift your posture from having fun to extreme focus. Now this was really a tough one for me, because I wanted to do everything but focus. However, to get me started on the right path, I wrote down a list of things that I wanted and needed to do; and I posted it on the inside of my bathroom mirror. As long as I remembered to brush my teeth and put on deodorant, I would always be reminded of my list.

What does it mean to be focused? Focus is defined (by Merriam-Webster' Dictionary) as "a center of activity, attraction, or attention; a point of concentration." Another way to put it is; you must remain steady and driven on a specific thing or task. Focus! Focus! Focus! I cannot stress it enough, it's so easy to allow your mind to drift off into LaLa land or take a mental vacation, but without focus you fail and if failure is present then success is nowhere in the picture. But somehow I think you would agree with me when I say that focus is definitely lacking in your plan and it's the chief enemy that's hindering your success. It's not that we don't desire to be just as successful as the next person and by no means are we short of great ideas and at times resources have been made available, but I, like you have trouble keeping my focus. We're faced with so many things that are vying for our attention (family, work, cell phones, recreation, social networks, etc.); it's no mystery why we remain stagnant in discovering our true inner creativity.

How many times have you had this crazy burst of energy to do something spectacular like start a business and make a life or career change, create a list of your life's goals or maybe even make a difference in your community? Then what's the next thing that happens? Your mind starts to wander and you think about all the effort and energy it's going to take to make it happen. So what do you do? You nestle back and think of something else that doesn't take much effort and/or energy. C'mon, I know I'm not out here by myself on this one: I know it's happened to you before as well. I am so easily distracted that anytime I start working on something I will allow my mind to wander into places that has absolutely nothing to do with my purpose or my destiny. I need to get it together-and so do you!

You Do The Math?

Take out a calculator and calculate the leisure time hours you spend at the mall, talking on the telephone, watching television, hanging with friends or just sitting around and then multiply that number by zero – once you've added it all up, tell me what it equals – you've guessed it,-**Nothing**. Each morning you should awaken with a plan charged up wanting to achieve more than you did on the day before. You started with great intentions of making it all happen but you become paralyzed by fear or failure and so you settle on doing absolutely nothing. You're expected to do greater things-so why aren't you?

How can we allow an emotion like fear paralyze us into sabotaging our destiny? How will you know what your future may bring if you're too afraid to step out into it? The acronym for "fear" is **F**alse **E**vidence **A**ppearing **R**eal. I'm no doctor, but fear that is allowed to linger for long periods of time can

sometimes open the door to health issues such as anxiety and panic attacks. I know this from my own personal experiences and when I learned how to exchange fearful thoughts with those of a positive nature, things got much better. For example, you're asked to speak at a public forum and as soon as your mind processes the thought you start getting nervous and your palms start to sweat. In order to overcome that gripping feeling of fear, you need to;
- **Immediately identify when it arrives.**
- **Know what in specific about it causes you to freeze up.**
- **Have a plan to deal with it head-on.**

But fear is even much more than that; it's a direct contradiction of what God said He was going to do in and through your life. Just for the record; God does not, cannot and will not ever contradict Himself. Now think about that for a moment, you're debating with God about what *He* said would take place in your life. That's Too Funny! I have no idea what instructions you were given for your life and how you were told to go about getting them accomplished, but it's never too late to search within yourself to find that out. Here's where the time you redeem daily in prayer and meditation could be very beneficial. Once you get into the habit of this self-discovery you will start challenging fear instead of fear challenging you. The only weapon that fear uses against you is that it creates a hint of impossibility and once you give into it-fear has you in its grip.

Where is your faith? Or maybe the question should be "do you have faith?" Whatever the case may be, know that faith and fear cannot dwell in the same place and you are at a pivotal point where a decision must be made on which will remain an active part of your daily living. Ask yourself, "Can I afford to continue doing nothing?" Doing nothing has a far greater price that will cost you so much more down the road. Remember, nothing in life is free! If you expect to reach your intended goal, you must commit one day out of the week working toward your goals until every week becomes everyday and everyday will eventually become every moment. And before you know it; your goals will become so embedded into your daily regimen, the only outcome would have to be a success. It's only when you reach this point that you will know you're making significant progress.

Are You Standing in the Same Spot?
Okay, I have a confession to make about a fascination that I have with crime shows, I don't know why but I enjoy watching CSI NY, City Confidential, Snapped, Criminal Minds, etc. You name it, I record it and on any given day I can easily spend 3-4 hours watching nothing but "crime-TiVo". And at the end of those 4 hours I feel so guilty about having wasted so much time on mindless television when I could have

been redeeming that time toward something of value, like my destiny and creating a legacy for my future generations. I'm not saying that you shouldn't occasionally watch television, listen to music or even go for walks to take a break, but when you find yourself giving more time to frivolous and unproductive things you're only further delaying your progress. You don't want to look back 5 or 10 years from now and face the realization that all of your time was wasted on unproductive activities. They were the kind of activities that only relaxed you but did not release you to your next level in life; they were fun but weren't fulfilling your purpose; they would tire you out but not transform you. If that time passes away and you're still standing in the same spot, you will have only yourself to blame for the lack of progress. Somehow, you have managed to convince yourself that you're making progress. Life for you right now is like walking 2 miles on a treadmill, your heart rate is up, you're sweating and boy are your legs tired, but guess what you did all of that and you haven't advanced anywhere. Sure, the workout display on the treadmill reads that you've walked 2 miles, but look around you're still in the same spot. You might be fooling those people around you with all the huffing and puffing, but when the treadmill stops and you get your workout summary, you'll find that the only person fooled is you. Wake up and start your life, get up (off your "you know what") and make things happen and move into your rightful position. It's your life and you're the only one qualified to live it.

Going In Circles
The older I get the more I've realized that the most valuable commodity I have is my time and that's the one thing that I cannot afford to waste or redeem casually. It's very easy to waste our time on mindless and fruitless activities when at the end of the day hasn't drawn us any closer to our destiny nor our purpose. You're probably asking yourself "What is my purpose? What is my destiny?" There is only one true way to know the answer to those questions and you must seek that direction from God. Jeremiah 1:5 says **"Before I formed you in the womb I knew you; before you were born I ordained you a prophet to the nations (NKJV)."** Do you know what God has ordained for you to become? Only God knows what He has called you to do in the earth and He is the only one who can truly lead you down that path. You know why, because He's the One with the map. You probably already know what it is you're supposed to be doing in life because you either spend a considerable amount of time avoiding or ignoring it, or it's something that you would wake up and do every day for free. I firmly believe that vision is one of the most important tools to success - and without vision you have no direction and without direction you will spend valuable time and resources going in endless circles.

A perfect example is Interstate 277 in Charlotte, NC. If you've ever driven on I-277 you would know that this stretch of interstate is an outer loop around uptown Charlotte. While on this loop you are given ample opportunities to exit into various parts of uptown and the city. There is also an exit that will drop you onto I-77 (north or south) which is one of the main interstates in the city. If my specific destination and purpose for traveling I-277 is to get me connected to I-77 south which takes me towards South Carolina, but I continue to travel on this loop because it's easy, I've memorized the route and it's an effortless drive. At some point, the journey will become mind draining and I would have burned a lot of gas, but guess what, if I were to keep this up I won't ever make it to my destination. This is what happens in most of our lives if we don't have a clear and defined plan for our lives.

If you expect to reach your intended goal(s) and attain your vision you must have a plan and it should be written down. You can start by purchasing a journal (you can call it –The Future of my Success) and write down your dreams, goals and aspirations. It may start out as a very short list, but as your vision increases so will your plan and as you expand your plan, the passion and desire that has remained hidden will begin to emerge. Creating a formal journal of your intended goals and keeping them in the forefront each day will keep you focused and hopefully heading in the right direction. Another option for you is to create what is called a "Vision Board." It requires a few inexpensive materials (scissors, poster board, glue and magazines), a relaxing atmosphere and an open mind. All you need to do is cut pictures and words from the magazine that best describes what you want to do, where you would like go and who you would like to meet and then paste this information in their respective categories. As you begin to see more of your vision on the board, the broader it will become. A search of the internet can assist you in getting started. Don't delay, it was one of the best things I could've ever done.

    Keep your goals visible by placing them in your journal, the list on your bathroom mirror, on the dashboard of your car or better yet, make it the wallpaper on your computer or cell phone. Huh, how about that for making the most out of modern technology. The two key culprits of an unfocused dreamer are lack of planning and procrastination and if you give either of them an inch of your time they will consume your life and absolutely devour your vision.

Focal Points for Vision:

- ➤ Am I making the most of my time? Is what I am about to do a core part of my vision and plan?

- ➤ Will it draw me closer to my purpose, calling or destiny in life?

- ➤ Are the people I am redeeming my (valuable) time with catapulting me towards my destiny?

- ➤ Is this activity going to "cause" me my success or "cost" me my success?

I guarantee that if you begin asking yourself these questions everyday throughout the day, it will change your course and lead you in the direction of a successful path.

Success Strategy:
1. Write your vision:

_____
_____
_____
_____
_____
_____
_____
_____

2. Complete the following statement: I will no longer be fearful of;

PASSION

WILL DRIVE IT!

Passion

What are you passionate about or what do you have a passion to do in life? It could be that you desire to enter into politics to be a positive voice in your community or maybe it's working with children and families in poverty or possibly a teacher, a doctor, lawyer or corporate executive. No matter what you aim to do in life it will definitely require passion to drive it. What is it that you crave, long, wish or yearn for, that every time you close your eyes it's all you can think about? It's described as a strong feeling of angst, strife or fear that at times you feel so trapped within yourself you could just explode. There are times when this feeling will even keep you awake at night or cause you to experience multiple daydreams in the middle of the day? Does this sound familiar? If so, then I've just described our next tool to get you on your path to success and that tool is Passion.

Passion is just as important to your plan as the very next breath you'll take. Without enough oxygen you will eventually die and without passion so does your vision and dreams. If you expect the plan and vision that God has given you to be manifested, you must be determined to breathe life into it every day. After your time with God your daily quiet time should be dedicated to your life plan. How is it that most of us will spend more time planning our Thanksgiving dinner, preparing our Christmas shopping lists, shoe shopping or personal pampering than we would planning for our personal and financial future?

You're at a point in this stage of your life where you must make the critical decision about what's important to you; your day-to-day mindless activities or the security of your financial future. I don't mind being transparent with you when I admit that I consistently evade the quiet and alone time that is necessary to really give adequate attention to my goals. So much so that I will give my time to others assisting them in achieving their goals and working toward making them a success just so that I won't have to work hard for myself. It's real easy to jump on the bandwagon of another person's plan, because they've already overcome the toughest hurdles, blood, sweat and tears. If you're familiar with the game of Double Dutch, you know that it takes less effort to stand in between the ropes and wait for them to turn than it does for you to follow the rhythm of the ropes to find the right time to jump in. Stop waiting around for the easy methods or quick solutions to come your way, waiting is what has you where you are currently - **NOWHERE**!

I remember being homebound for a few weeks after having major surgery. And during my quiet time with God, He revealed to me very clearly that I was blatantly avoiding working my own vision and by avoiding it I was showing Him that I did not trust Him to make the vision come to pass. That revelation gave me the necessary insight as to why my goals had not made it to the finish line. In that instant I knew what I had to do; and that was to take a step back from a lot of the extra and non-essential activities that I had joined myself to and re-direct my time and energy to my own projects. Whatever you have yourself connected to, make sure all points lead back to fulfilling your vision.

With that being said, you're going to have to become more accustomed to saying "**NO**." Go ahead, say it with me again; "**NO**." Didn't that feel wonderful? At times, "NO" is the best response you could ever give and you shouldn't feel bad about having to say it. It does not matter who's doing the asking; anyone is capable of attempting to distract you and steer you off course. You shouldn't even consider the request if it has nothing to do with implementing your future plans or vision.

Do you think Michael Jordan, President Barak Obama, Oprah Winfrey or Will Smith would be where they are today had they entertained distractions or just sat around hoping that success would drop into their laps. They identified with their major passion (basketball, politics, acting, journalism & music) and stayed with their plan, sacrificed leisure time, tuned out the naysayers and minimized distractions. This disciplined behavior showed their friends and family they were serious about their journey and nothing would stop them from getting there. These individuals are not limited to only their major passions; they are satisfied with where their minor passions have taken them as well. In making similar sacrifices you will discover that you're passionate about more than one thing too, but the key to avoid getting frustrated is that you must identify which one stands out over the others and begin working with just that one. If you're not sure where to begin, I would recommend writing a list of those things you're passionate about and next to each item write a brief description as to why you are passionate about that thing and what you would do given the opportunity to fulfill it. After looking over the list and their descriptions, you should be able to determine almost immediately which of the passions you should begin cultivating.

Getting a Leg Up

As I mentioned in the previous chapter, I enjoy watching any type of crime TV and I've seen numerous episodes where the criminals are running from the police and (it never fails) they always seem to meet that preverbal wall or fence that stands between their getting caught or getting away from the police. Instantly, they're faced with a decision as to who should be the first to go over and who might remain behind and risk the possibility of getting caught. In that instance (depending on why they're running) a decision is made based on who is the most determined of the duo and which of the two stands to lose the most if they're captured. Then they must decide which one will assist the other over their present hurdle. I would often wonder if once the first person was able to achieved their freedom as a result of their friend or partner, would they turn back to give the other person a lift over as well. I'm quite sure that you are not evading the law; at least I hope not but are you evading your vision and delaying your personal success. To be honest, that was something for me to think about because I actually was evading mine by always assisting others in achieving their goals, while in the back of my mind wondering if they would be there for me when I needed to get a leg up over my hurdles. That's why it is so important to know early on who has your back and will they be there to support you when you reach those hurdles or low points on your journey. I am not suggesting that you take a selfish approach and not assist a fellow friend or family member in need of your gifting or skill set, but the moral here is to watch and know who you're running with. Don't get me wrong, it's not a bad thing to help another person realize their dream; just make sure that everyone involved has pure motives, good intentions and you'll be able to continue to count on each other when or if the time comes. Just keep in mind that the help you end up receiving may not come from the same individual, so be open to whomever or wherever it may come. There will come a time when you'll need something specific to advance your dream to the next level and that need won't be met by the person you assisted; it's going to come from the most unlikely candidate. You could possibly possess the skill of internet research while the other person may be excellent at making cold calls and speaking with the public. Whatever skills and talents you each possess, I think it is acceptable to give them a reasonable amount of your time. But whatever you do, don't get off task.

Having Your Vision in Sight

Imagine you're in a group that's stranded on a desert island and it's been almost 2 weeks since any of you have had food and water. When suddenly, you discover what appears to be water from afar and you start imaging how refreshing it would be to just taste it. Your strategy is to figure out how you will get to it and what you're going to do once you get it in your hands. Now the real question is, "just how thirsty are you?" and "how bad do you want it? You realize that competition exists and obstacles are evident since you are not the only one going after the much needed sustenance, but it will be all worthwhile in the end. You should know that you are not the only one that was given this particular plan that you have; however, you are the only one that has been assigned to bring it to pass during this time and season. So don't get it twisted, you can waste time wishing and hoping if you want to, but if you sleep on this, the next person will make it happen and they will be telling the success story that should have been told by you. While in the process of writing this book, I experienced all kinds of distractions tempting me to hang out with my friends, lounge by the pool, go to the movies or attend concerts, but I had to keep reminding myself of the deadline I had set for the completion of this project. Did I want to go out and engage in those things? Yes, but I had reached a certain level where success was in sight, so I had to keep moving towards it. The future of your success is likened to the desire of trying to reach that water before anyone else, you've got to be moving when everyone else is still, working while others are vacationing and being watchful while they're asleep. You cannot attain your goals and bring forth your vision with a casual or leisure mindset; you have to want it with every fiber in you-as if your life depended on it. And it does!

When vision and passion intersect you can't allow "anyone or anything" to prevent you from reaching that intended goal and you must allow God's manifested purpose to be revealed in you. Paul said in Philippians 3:14; "**I press toward the goal for the prize of the upward call of God in Christ Jesus (NKJV).**" The goal that God has for your life should totally absorb your energy. I would advise that you wake up each day asking God this question, "what is Your purpose and Your plan for my life today?" Our lives are daily loaded with His benefits (*Psalm 68:19*) and if we line up with His plan we have a right to reap those benefits. For instance, the benefits in your insurance plan states that you're only eligible for generic prescriptions, but you always want the pharmacist to fill the prescription using the brand. Well guess what, you can get the brand prescription but they are not going to pay for anything outside of the benefits established in your plan. So why do we expect God to move or do anything outside of His plan and benefits. It's a privilege we definitely do not deserve but we should be willing to walk it out and see our vision as He sees it. If you diligently seek Him, He will respond and before you know it you'll find yourself walking out the calling He has for your life.

Focal Points for Passion;
- Discover your major and minor passions.

- Dedicate time and energy toward the future of your success?

- Recognize and minimize your distractions.

- Are you reaping all of the benefits?

Success Strategy:
1. I will commit to at least _____ hours per week planning and conducting research for my vision.

2. What non-essential commitments and activities will you now have to say "no" to in order to advance your vision?
   _____
   _____
   _____

3. Which of the passions from your list have you decided to focus and cultivate? And Why?
   _____
   _____

MOTIVATION

KEEPS IT ALIVE!

Motivation

Chaos! I know it sounds strange, but I am motivated by chaos. Many of the major projects that I've accomplished in the past started out in chaos. If you were to give me a task or project that nobody wanted and provide me with the freedom to be creative; I will expend all of my time and energy into getting it done. If it doesn't keep me thinking and moving, I will be swallowed up by boredom.

Motivation is a key player in your quest for success and unless you get the unction to move nothing will happen. Simply put, motivation is described as stimulus or influence. What is it that motivates you to get out of bed in the morning, play competitive sports, relocate to a new city, buy a new house or car, get married and/or start a family? We're all faced with similar questions in our lifetime but we each will respond to them in different ways, because for most; our depleted motivation is based on our past experiences, low self-esteem, lack of encouragement and present life circumstances. If you've ever been told that you're not smart enough, you don't have what it takes or you'll never amount to anything, you can rest assured that your level of motivation will be low. If you're striving to become a wealthy and successful individual, you'll learn very quickly that money can be a strong motivating factor. Meaning, if making money is the only reason you have for realizing your dream then you may have to reevaluate your decision. There has to be something else to keep you going when business is slow or not turning a profit. For example, if you were to open a restaurant in a high traffic tourist town, you are sure to make lots of money from new customers visiting for the first time, but what about having a plan to keep the repeat business and possibly have your restaurant featured in a local or national travel magazine. Here is where motivation to "grow" the business would intervene. Money shouldn't be your only motivating factor in what you are called to do because if it is, once you've acquired the funds or reached your monetary goal, whatever you plan to do next is still going to require another level of drive to keep it alive. Think about the feeling you get on the morning of a half workday and it's a Friday the week before you're scheduled to go on vacation. As opposed to the feeling you have the night before returning to work from your nice long vacation. On that Friday you're in a good mood and excited, very sociable and even motivated to get work done that you've been avoiding all week. Your adrenaline is pumped so high, not even your boss' bad mood could stop this feeling. It's a natural high and you don't want to come down from it too prematurely. Does this happy feeling I've just described sound familiar? If so, then you understand that your plan will require the same type of energy, enthusiasm and you've got to find a way to preserve it all for future use.

In my opinion money should be the last item on your checklist to secure. I know it sounds like a crazy thing to say, but if you were to have immediate access to funding without a solid plan, it would be disastrous and a future train wreck waiting to happen. In some cases, it might be fairly easy to get your hands on the cash needed to start your business, but having a solid plan will keep the business viable and moving. If you expect to be successful at anything, there has to be something other than money to motivate you every day. It's the kind of motivation that get's you out of bed early and keeps you up late at night.

Shifting from "Neutral"
Get out of the "Neutral" position and shift into "Drive" better yet-Overdrive! In other words, take that long awaited leap of faith and be willing to take a risk to realize your dreams. I'm sure you're familiar with the sayings "no risk, no reward' or "no pain, no gain". These (and many others) are not just cute pep talk expressions; they're real and so is the outcome if you continue to take an inactivate role in your own life. Neutral is a safe position which allows you to sit in the driver's seat, with your foot on the brakes, buckled up, GPS data locked in and even turning the steering wheel making revved up engine sounds. But it's not until you shift from neutral to drive that you'll start moving from a still stagnant position to steering towards your future. Everybody wants to remain hidden and safe within their own comfort zones, but

the last time I checked success was not a one person show; you have to take risks if you're going to reap the rewards. The ability for you to stay motivated could be in getting connected and building relationships outside of your safe circle.

There's no need for you to take off at a top rate of speed, just take your time and try not to rush through it. Depending on the goal you're aiming for, it could take anywhere from a month to 5 years to complete. So it doesn't matter how long it takes to get there, the key is that you finish and you finish strong. I'm almost certain that you didn't learn how to drive, understand the rules of the road and obtain a driver's license all in one day, so don't expect to accomplish success so quickly. For some, success may come easy and for others it is going to involve hard work and dedication. However you arrive at your pinnacle of success motivation is what's needed to keep it alive and thriving.

Fueling Your Passion

Motivation is the fuel needed for your passion and desire. Without the fuel of motivation your passion will remain in the daydreaming phase and eventually your vision and plan will cease to exist. The engine of motivation should be so revved up that it becomes difficult to sleep, eat or do anything other than working toward your vision. You'll get to the point where you are totally consumed with your vision that your conversations will change, you'll engage in more productive activities and the people you redeem time with will be springboards to that vision. Keep in mind, motivation comes in many different forms and it's important to know the "motivation fuel type" needed to get you going. Does your motivation run on diesel or unleaded? If we were referencing an automobile, the fuel type would make a huge difference. If you were to put diesel fuel into an unleaded fuel tank, it will ride, but eventually it will damage your engine and cause all sorts of other problems with your vehicle. The same thing happens with your success if you're fueling it with little or no quiet time, lack of resources, prayer and most of all a negative environment.

What do you think the probability of success would be if a basketball were to be used during the Super Bowl or what's the likelihood of becoming a successful tennis player if your motivation is fueled by roller-skating. I'll answer that for you, it would be low to nearly non-existent and it just won't happen. You must focus on those things that will get you where you want to go and it's going to take intense dedication to the process to get there. Having a strategic plan in place to keep you moving during those low motivational periods will prevent fewer distracting pit-stops and instead will force you to stay on your projected course and meet your desired goals.

Motivation is the unexplainable influence that exists within us and forces us to do extraordinary things and make certain decisions that will drive us toward our pre-ordained purpose.

Motivation will;
- Keep you at home on a Friday night conducting research for your business.
- Have you turning off your cell phone so that you can focus on creating your business plan.
- Have you attending conferences and seminars instead of concerts and the movies.

When you start noticing your lifestyle and interests have taken a swift turn, that's when you'll know your motivation has kicked into overdrive. I recognized something had changed with me as soon as I found myself reading more books and spending more time at the library and less time in front of the television. If you haven't done so already, I strongly encourage you to read "Who Moved My Cheese, by Dr. Spencer Johnson." This is a story about change and how you adapt to it; and in my opinion what it is that motivates you to either move forward or stand still. The force and energy behind motivation will push or pull you in either direction; the choice of where it leads is up to you. You'll either be motivated to lounge around on the sofa watching television and eating junk food or you'll be motivated to take charge over your life and cause change to occur.

Make a decision right now to choose a specific day in the week where you start devoting constructive time to your goals and over the course of time watch how they materialize right before your eyes. No longer should you allow outside influences such as family, friends and self doubt distract you and take you off course. There are some people in your life who will want to see you succeed and will cheer you on along the way and others will do all they can to watch and wait for you to fail. Don't waste time and energy worrying about whose with you or whose against you, you'll recognize them by the way they encourage or discourage you and whether they are drawing near to hinder you or giving you the space and time needed to make it happen. If their presence and input is not a catapulting agent of your progress then, in love, you have the right to put distance between you and them. You have a destiny to be fulfilled and it requires you staying on track, you'll have time for them later. Friends and family are the leading contributors of "destroying the destiny" in their loved one's life, but as a future success story you cannot, shall not, and better not allow anyone to keep you from reaching your point in destiny. I cannot stress enough the importance of creating a vision board or posting a photo of your dream home or car, desired vacation spot or your vision/mission statement somewhere where you will encounter them every day. These visible objects will keep the motivation alive and your goals in sight.

Name That Tune

It doesn't matter who you are or where you were raised we all have a love for the sound of music. Whether you like it very loud (like me) or very soft, soothing and relaxing-you just know that you like your style and preference of music. I enjoy almost any genre of music from Classical to Old School Rap; it's something about music that ignites me and gets me moving. One of my all time favorite "get me going" song is "I'm Every Woman" performed by Whitney Houston. I don't care where I am, whose around or what I'm doing, I will break out singing and even dancing. It's something about the lyrics in this song that seem to motivate me. The lyrics are; *"I'm every woman, it's all in me. Anything that you want done baby, I'll do it naturally"* and another verse says, *"I ain't braggin cause I'm the one. You just ask me and it shall be done. And don't bother to compare cause I've got it."* These lyrics describe how I feel about me and it gives me the feeling I can take on the world. It also reminds me that no one can do what I do better than me. What's your tune? Go ahead, pop it in your CD player or download it to your IPod© and just let it play. Music is not only inspiring it's also influencing.

Focal Points for Motivation:
- Identify motivating factors that will drive me towards success.
- Devote quality time towards my vision and goals.
- Post a visual list to keep me motivated.
- Name That Tune & Play It!

<u>Success Strategy:</u>

1. List the circumstances in your life (past or present) that have affected your ability to be motivated and/or have confidence?

   _____
   _____
   _____

2. Ok it happened or it was said, so what are "you" going to do to change how "you "see yourself? It could be that you may need to lovingly confront the person who hurt you and forgive them.

   _____
   _____
   _____

3. Now Get Motivated!

EDUCATION

WILL CULTIVATE IT!

Education

Scholars would have you to ascribe to the idea that you need to have a degree from an accredited college or university in order to be successful. I agree with their reasoning but only to a certain extent because that's not always the case. Success is not a respecter of a college degrees or your high school diploma. Success and entrepreneurship are for those who are hungry for change and want to totally dismiss mediocrity. However, you will find (as I have) that the wages you earn are deeply affected by your level of education or lack thereof. I know this scenario all too well. Every employer I've ever worked for I've always excelled at any task that I was given and my performance appraisals were usually a clear indication of this fact. However, when promotion time came around they would always say, "you interviewed well," we find you to be a great asset to the company," "your quality of work is great and you're an awesome team player," and "you get along well with others, everyone seems to like you." Then comes that preverbal, "but" we've decided to go with another candidate and you find out later that the other candidate was merely hired because they had gone to college and acquired a degree of some sort. Has this ever happened to you? If you've experienced this form of discrimination in your salary, as I have with my current and previous employers; you were most likely paid less because you did not have a high school diploma or a college degree. This can be one of the most hurtful, frustrating and debilitating feelings that one can experience and I've felt all of those emotions at some point or another. However, despite what they may say and what you've earned; don't let that negative talk and mindset keep you from your attempts of pursuing your intended success. Let me tell you something, you don't need to have degrees on the wall or letters behind your name to be considered a success, but you *will* have to educate yourself in the industry of the business you plan to enter into.

You Can Do It Too!

I particularly like the success story of Bill Gates, the Founder and CEO of Microsoft©. It was at the early age of 13 when he realized he had a passion for computer programming and even wrote his very first computer program. He and four other students of his school were hired by a local company to find bugs in the company's software. The administrator's at his school took notice of his abilities with computers and programming, and offered him an opportunity to write the school's program for their students' schedules. Gates went on to graduate from high school, attended Harvard University and during that time he experienced many other minor successes until he hit the biggest one of all in 1979, Microsoft©. He experienced all of this success at a young age and guess what, he had not graduated from Harvard and had not received a degree at the time of his success with Microsoft©. I believe Bill Gates had the vision (Focus), passion and motivation needed to bring the vision of Microsoft© to pass and a formal education was just a small part of his success.

Allow me to introduce you to a few other millionaires who became successful without obtaining a college degree;

- **Mary Kay Ash** - The founder of Mary Kay Inc. Her cosmetic brand is known around the world.

- **Simon Cowell** – Started out working in the mailroom at a record company and now American Idol has made him a household name.

- **Michael Dell** – He had $1,000, dedication and desire & created Dell, Inc. You can find his computers and laptops in homes and offices around the globe.

- **Steve Jobs** - Only attended a semester of college and worked at Atari before co-founding Apple Computers. His innovation has made the IPod© and the Ipad© the latest craze.

You, just like those previously mentioned and the many other success stories that have contributed to the advancement of our society, had to start where they were at that time. This success can occur while you're currently unemployed or while working for someone else. There is never a perfect time to start a business, so quit telling yourself that you'll move forward with your plans once you finish school, or when the kids go off to college, or once you've saved up enough money. For every reason you give yourself not to start there are a dozen more reasons why you should. I encourage you to learn more about these individuals as well as others like them. Spending time reading Inc, Money and Forbes magazine's opened me up to a whole new world of innovation, entrepreneurship and success; and someday they'll be publishing my success story and yours too. You can see those whom I've mentioned took different strides to get to where they are now but guess what; THEY MADE IT-AND SO WILL YOU!

     How much do you know about what it is that you plan to do? Have you conducted any online research, read any books or conducted a market analysis? While having a plan, vision and motivation are great tools to possess, educating yourself about your venture is vitally important to your continued growth and success in that industry. I am not suggesting you go out right now and register in a 2 or 4 year accredited college, but I am suggesting you look into taking courses such as Business Administration, Basic Accounting, Basic Marketing, Business Plan Writing and Free Resources, etc. that are being offered at your local community college. These courses and resources can assist you in knowing how to put your plan on paper and get you to asking the right questions to move you forward and asking those that you didn't even know you should be asking.

Knowledge is Power, Power is Influence, and Influence is Leadership!

Make Time to Make Money

Another way you can educate yourself in a chosen industry is to surround yourself with people who have worked in that industry and have succeeded at overcoming failure. Whoa! Now there's a word that no one likes to hear – FAILURE! Don't kid yourself into thinking that as soon as you get that grand idea you'll be an instant success. You best believe that behind every positive success story there are definitely a ton of failures that preceded it. I've dabbled in many different ventures from selling Tupperware© to Real Estate, you name it and I've tried it. And with each one I anticipated great success, but when one venture didn't work out, it only motivated me to keep searching for what I was supposed to be doing. But there's one thing I've learned through all of this and that was "giving up is not an option." You see, giving up is easy and it doesn't take much effort to convince yourself that you cannot or should not do it and before you know it, you've talked yourself out of your destiny. Whatever your plans are, you shouldn't plan on doing it alone; try finding a mentor or an accountability partner who is willing to work with you. Having these resourceful influences in your life is crucial to your sanity, they're the ones who will talk you down off that ledge of "quit and give up" and encourage you to continue moving forward. If "procrastination" is a common hindrance of mine then next in line would be the "lone ranger" syndrome, trying to do it all by myself without asking for help or advice. I'll work triple times over before I take time to ask a question, and I believe it's that very attitude of stubbornness that kept me from being successful in real estate. During this period of my life I was not only attempting to sell real estate, I also held a full-time and part-time job. I was attempting to do it all and had never taken the time to sit down with a seasoned real estate professional to assist me with managing my time and navigating through the business. What is the likelihood of mastering the skill of planting & growing bananas if you're spending a majority of your time hanging out with tobacco farmers? It's not possible, because the instructions as well as the outcome will be very different. So if you're hanging out with friends and family members who are not planting seeds of success in your life then over the course of time you'll only end up with weeds. Having someone around that has been there and done that is vital to operating successfully.

There is term that is frequently used in the insurance industry called LKQ; which stands for Like, Kind and Quality. And what's meant by this term is, instead of the insurance company spending money on you receiving a new part for your vehicle, they will cover the cost of a LKQ part. This in a nutshell is an experienced part that has previously served the purpose in which you have a need of right now. My point is you don't have to reinvent the wheel in whatever you're attempting to put your hands to, because there is a LKQ partner waiting to catapult you into your success.

    As you move forward with your planning, you'll learn that the resources of people at times will far outweigh financial resources. Make no mistake about it, you will definitely need funding to get your business started but the resources of people will provide you with the direction that's needed on how to not only apply for funding but advise you on how to budget and spend it wisely. And since they have more industry experience than you, they can offer wisdom on obtaining funding from sources other than the traditional lending institutions. It's extremely important to include time in your schedule for volunteer work alongside a business coach or mentor. Your coach or mentor will assist you with understanding the ins and outs of the business and it will only cost you a few hours a week. Sacrificing time and energy in the onset will prove to be very valuable in the long run. You'll be surprised at how much you can learn about your future success via "sweat equity." In other words, free labor.

Knowledge is Valuable

The more you know the more you'll grow. I know it sounds a little elementary, but it makes a whole lot of sense. Your quest for knowledge can begin by searching the internet for various seminars and workshops specific to your industry or interests. You will not only acquire a wealth of general information, but it will also broaden your resources and connect you with others in that same field. The key to "education" is gaining valuable knowledge, wisdom and insight from those with more experience than you. Remember, you're not going to always receive education in the traditional classroom setting, so you must broaden your methods and expectations of learning. I'm sure you're convinced that your brilliant idea or concept is going to change how we currently do business or maybe even the world, but the most heinous mistake you could ever make is to think you can do it alone and you know all there is to know about succeeding in this specific area.

Snap out of it! You don't know everything, you've got to ask questions and realize that you're never too old to learn something new. I know you may not like what I'm saying, but anyone who finds themselves in direct contradiction to the above statement can be perceived as stubborn and even arrogant.

Like I've said before, there's absolutely nothing wrong with obtaining a formal education from a college or business school and grabbing a few degrees while you're at it, but don't let the fact that you don't have a college degree trip you up and keep you from stepping into a new dimension of your life and future.

The Competition
Valuable and countless hours have been spent learning about your specific industry or interests, educating and preparing yourself for that glorious road to success. It won't matter how much you learn or how comfortable you feel with your preparation for the known and unknown obstacles, there is still another aspect of your business you will need to learn. And that is, your competition. You can consider them to be your direct or indirect competition, you will still have to familiarize yourself with their product, their company structure and what makes your product and/or service better than theirs. The leader of a military troop would never consider invading their enemy's camp without a strategic battle plan, a map of their territory and locating the weak spots on how to defeat them and you should consider adopting the same process when it comes to your competition.

Focal Points for Education:
- Make an investment in learning by taking courses and attending seminars.
- Volunteer time to learn about your industry or interests.
- Ask! Ask! Ask! Don't be afraid to ask questions.
- Knowledge is Power, Power is Influence and Influence is Leadership!
- Study Your Competition.

Success Strategy:
1. Write a brief sentence describing what you've learned about your chosen industry/career. Why have you chosen this particular area of interest?

   _____
   _____
   _____
   _____

2. I plan to subscribe, purchase or borrow the following books and/or magazines to educate me on my area of interest:

   _____
   _____
   _____

3. I have decided to work with _____ as my mentor and accountability partner.

FUNDING

PROVIDES FOR IT!

Funding

    We have arrived at the point in our journey that no one ever wants to deal with or they experience difficulty in knowing the exact direction they should take. Whenever I thought about the funding needed for my various projects, the feeling of fear and anxiety would instantly paralyze me and I would totally shut the idea down at that time. I consider the thought of acquiring funding to be like a lasso choking the life out of your vision, business ideas and any of your dreams or aspirations. You choke up and almost lose your breath at the mere thought of asking for money to fund your business.

    During the cowboy era a lasso was typically used to wrestle cattle and villains in order to keep them from getting away. They would start off by circling the rope above their head and when they felt the cattle was getting too far ahead of them; the cowboy would lasso the cattle, tighten up on the grip and stop them dead in their tracks. The paralyzing thought of dealing with a lender or investor can and will do the same thing to your success. Everything is "peachy keen" when you're talking about your dreams, creating your business plan and even having meetings and networking, but as soon as you begin dealing with how the venture will be funded, that's when the mental "lasso grip" stops you dead in your tracks. (Revisit the section on "Vision" to see how you should handle fear when it arises.) Let's face it; money is a difficult topic of discussion for anyone regardless of who you're having this conversation with. So if you want to make this a little easier on yourself, the first item on your agenda should be to calculate the amount of money needed and then explain how you plan to use it. Based on this snapshot of information it will determine the funding source you need to consider borrowing from.

There are four standard sources in which you can obtain funding from, but you should know their minimal requirements and what they'll be expecting from you. They are as follows and we'll briefly discuss each one;

- ***Family & Friends***
- ***Lending Institutions***
- ***Venture Capitalists***
- ***Angel Investors***

Family and Friends

Depending on the amount of the investment, utilizing close friends & family to fund your venture is a great first step. However, I would caution you to make sure it has been clearly establish whether the funds are a gift or a loan. You'll definitely want to confirm they are willing to accept the risks that come with making this type of investment and the terms of the return (dividends) are clearly expressed at the onset of the initial agreement. If this is handled improperly, you stand a chance of damaging very valuable relationships. Another viable consideration would be to send out a Sponsorship Letter to at least 50 or 100 of your closest friends and family asking them to make a small non-equity investment into your start up expenses. You'll find that there are people who want to invest in you and they'll ask for nothing in return.

Lending Institutions

Your local bank is the most common source for funding but they're usually the most difficult. When planning to borrow money from a bank they'll usually require you to have excellent credit, a complete business plan with market analysis, industry experience, collateral and other pertinent documentation. And other factors are the amount of your loan request, your plans for the funds and how they will be repaid. If the bank perceives that they're unable to assist you with the necessary funding because the risk is too high or the return is too low, they may recommend you contact your local Small Business Administration (www.sba.gov) to see if you would qualify with them for a small business loan. Don't be discouraged if they turn you away, a SBA loan may be the best thing for you.

Venture Capitalists

Venture Capitalists (VC) are investors who invest in business ventures providing capital for start-ups or expansions. Venture capitalists are looking for a higher rate of return than would be given by traditional investors. Most venture capital investments are made in cash with the understanding that there will be an exchange for shares in the invested company. It is typical for venture capital investors to identify and back companies in high technology industries such as biotechnology and IT, but depending on the rate of return they are known to invest in other lucrative business opportunities. Before submitting to the idea of this type of funding, you will want to conduct in depth research on their requirements and what would be their expectations from you. You may be asked to turn over a percentage of your company and you would want to be aware of this before signing any agreement.

Angel Investors

Angel investors or an Angel is an affluent individual who provides capital for a business start-up, usually in exchange for convertible debt or ownership equity. Angel investors are an organized group or network of angels who share research and pool their investment capital in a variety of business opportunities. Angel investors are similar to venture capitalists in their regard for a rate of return on their investment, but they will often be a little more flexible in their minimum amount to invest and their types of investments may vary.

Whichever source you choose to fund your vision, I recommend that you thoroughly research the pros and cons of using that source. You'll also want to check with your local Better Business Bureau (www.bbb.org) to find out if any complaints have been filed or better yet make sure that the organization is not currently under investigation.

Focal Points for Funding:
- Don't become paralyzed by the thought of applying for a loan.
- Explore the best funding option for your business.
- Know exactly how much is needed and more importantly how you will repay.
- Utilize the resources of the Small Business Administration and the Better Business Bureau.

Success Strategy:

1. What is the minimal amount that I will need to get my business started $_____$?

2. How much capital do I have or will I have as an initial investment $_____$?

3. I plan to ask the following friends and family to make a start-up investment; _____, _____, and _____.

TAKING ACTION

WILL MANIFEST IT!

Taking Action

Now that you have written your vision, passion is present, motivation is alive and education and funding have been lined up, the next thing you've got to do is "*Take Action*." That means, get up, do something, stop wishing and quit complaining. It's not the responsibility of your parents, your spouse or your best friend to put legs to your plan-IT'S ALL ON YOU! How are you going to get from where you are right now to where you are supposed to be? And are you prepared for the length of time it may take and what you will have to give up in the process. When you make the decision to "take action" you're actively engaging in the process. Building a business is much like farming to the degree that it involves digging, planting and pruning. Digging would represent the extensive research required. Planting symbolizes you building positive and healthy relationships that will cultivate the growth of your business. Pruning is the act of cutting away the personal and professional hindrances affecting your growth & prosperity. Your plan of action begins with creating a To Do List or depending on the extent of your goal; a Project Tracker to help keep you on schedule. Don't overwhelm yourself by trying to take on the entire list all at once, that's a sure way to give up before you even start. This At-A Glance checklist will serve as target point reminders, so limit your details and keep it fairly simple. My personal plan consisted of typing a simple checklist that consisted of key vision and motivational milestones. Having a checklist accessible at all times forced me to keep my vision in perspective, because if I didn't everything else that was to follow in my plan just wouldn't work. It's imperative to stay on track with your plan and that's going to include making huge sacrifices along with clear-cut lifestyle changes. I'd rather lose a little now in order to gain more in the long run.

<u>Making the Connection</u>
All of this probably won't make much sense to your friends and family, so don't be upset if they're unable to see and understand it right away. They all weren't meant to catch your vision, only you were. Besides, this may be the point in time of your journey where you will just have to go it alone for a while. God already knows who sincerely supports you and wants to witness your success, so He must shield you from the people who can hurt you the most. If this should happen to you, then you need to find a place of peace, calm and resolve within yourself to know that it's okay for you to move forward without them and when, or if they get on board you will know for sure if they're the right relationship(s) to remain connected with. On the flipside of that, they can't see the entire vision because you've only been given a glimpse of it yourself; because there is another piece of the puzzle you still need to connect with in order to arrive at the final conclusion.

That's exactly what happened during the discovery and invention of the Post-it-Note, the adhesive stationary that changed the way we bookmark. Arthur Fry and Spencer Silver were scientists and inventors working for 3M®. Spencer Silver was a chemist at 3M® who accidentally invented a low tack reusable adhesive. For many years he tried to promote it through his company and his seminars but they were not interested in the idea at the time. Arthur Fry would occasionally attend Silver's seminars. As the legend goes, Fry was in church when he came up with the perfect application. Fry sang in his church choir on weekends, and would use slips of paper to mark the pages of his hymnal. When the book was opened, however, the makeshift bookmarks often moved around or fell out altogether. One Sunday in 1974, it occurred to him that Silver's reusable adhesive could be put to use to create a better bookmark. If it could be coated on paper, Silver's adhesive would hold a bookmark in place without damaging the page on which it was placed. The next day, Fry requested a sample of the re-usable adhesive. He began experimenting, coating only one edge of the paper so that the portion extending from a book would not be sticky. Fry used some of his experiments to write notes to his boss. This use led him to broaden his original idea into the concept that we now know as the infamous Post-it note. So as you can see, both Fry and Silver had a vision to discover success with their inventions, but it wasn't until they brought their ideas together that success was achieved.

<u>Don't Get Derailed</u>

When your plans are in motion and on the right track nothing you encounter should be able to derail you. Your plan of action is your destiny road map and every pivotal point on the map will have a level of achievement assigned to it. For instance, a specific task or benchmark that is tied to your destiny road map is at the six month mark, and it's at that point where you should be able to see yourself achieving new levels of success towards your ultimate goal. My visual road map was a whiteboard that hung in my office next to my computer and I would write down key actions and deadlines I wanted to make. Every time I would remove an action from my whiteboard it encouraged me even more to continue pressing forward. **COMPLETION! SATISFACTION! SUCCESS!** If a small step to success is attached to every benchmark; it will give you the energy, motivation and encouragement needed to continue pressing forward. Halfway through your journey you'll look back and witness the success milestones and hurdles you've crossed and this will boost the passion and motivation you're going to need for the next level. The closer you are to reaching those goals in your plan of action the easier it will become. One of the toughest things you will experience on this journey is the energy to just get started, but once you do and you begin building your momentum you'll discover that not even "_you_" can stop "_you_" from reaching the next level.

Doubt, fear, hesitation and all sorts of second guessing will rear their ugly heads, but you must remind them that you're in control. NOTHING is going to hold you back. Never let the emotion of fear and the thought of failure push aside your passion. There are going to be times when you'll doubt yourself, your plan and the vision you see and you will even want to give up, but you have to keep resonating in your mind the end reward. If you choose to stop now and give up you will only put yourself further behind and be forced to start from that stopping point or maybe even worse, from the beginning-and I know you really don't want to do that. Your action plan should definitely include having a plan to counteract any attacks the naysayers will try to inflict upon you and the ones you might even inflict upon yourself. It might be a great idea to have your favorite quote, scripture or an accountability partner available when those moments do arise. Believe me you will definitely need to have someone or something nearby to talk you down off of that ledge of fear. At times, you will find yourself standing on that ledge trying to back out or thinking of all kinds of reasons why you don't believe that you're qualified to do it, but instantly you must decide who is going to win; you or the fear.

No Breakdowns Allowed

You have come to understand that fear is false evidence appearing real and even more so it's a contradiction of the truth about what God is calling you to do. So it's okay if you entertain the thought of fear for a brief moment, but **ONLY FOR A MOMENT.** After that minute is up you've got to "keep it moving" and learn how to speak to that fear and doubt and cast if from the level of authority it's trying to have in your life and over your destiny.

Taking Action will also include a period of rest where you pause to take a mental and physical break. Your mind and body will go into overload and without periodic recharges; you just might cause a mental and/or physical breakdown. Think of it in the same way you would if you were preparing to take a road trip and all the preventive maintenance that you would do in order to avoid a breakdown on the road. If your car were to breakdown, it typically would not happen directly in front of the service station. It's usually going to be in the most unlikely and inconvenient place. Well the same thing can occur at a critical point in your journey. Your mind and body will appreciate the break and who knows, it could be the break you need to reload and refresh on new ideas and expound on the ideas and plans that you currently have in place. It would be a big mistake to think that God has shown you the entire vision all at once. In some cases He may do that but for the most part, He only shows you in part, and that way you will be reminded about how you need to abide in Him in order for the full manifestation of the vision to come to pass.

Viewing Success in 3D –Desire, Drive & Discipline

If you've ever been to a movie that was made with the 3D effect, you will know that once you put on the 3D glasses, it brings the movie so close that you think you can actually reach out and touch it. I can't quite recall the name of the movie I first saw in 3D, but I can remember the experience of feeling like the characters were as close as the person sitting in front of me. But when I removed the 3D glasses, I was reminded of how far away I was from the screen. These glasses really came in handy if you were sitting in the back of the theatre. Well, viewing your success in 3D is a little different than watching the movie because you can control how close your success is and how long it remains there.

Your view of success is a matter of your own personal perspective. It's not important what others think of you, but what you think of yourself. Listening to and believing what God is saying to you about you is the only opinion that matters. Wait a minute! I want you to do something with me. Grab your best looking shades and put them on. Now close your eyes for 10 seconds and imagine your success in the following 3D image;

Desire – If you don't carry a desire to see something miraculous happen in your own life, then it won't happen. If you walk around with that "ho-hum" attitude then you'll receive a "ho-hum" outcome.

Drive – You've got to put some legs to your plan. It's beautiful on paper and even perfect when you sit and daydream about it, but until it can get up and walk and make a difference then life will continue to sit still.

Discipline – It has been said that it takes 21 days to break a habit, so whatever has been keeping you from fulfilling your destiny and purpose, avoid "that" very thing for 21 days. If you can commit to doing that then you are well on your way to success.

Focal Points for Taking Action:
- Don't allow friends and family to distract you.
- Set bench marks on your Destiny Road Map.
- Get yourself an accountability partner, someone to keep you motivated.
- View it in 3D Desire, Drive and Discipline.

Success Strategies:

1. I will no longer allow _____, _____, and _____ to be distractions from my plan.

2. By _____/_____/_____ I will have completed my _____ and will be able to move forward to _____ which is the next phase of my plan.

3. List what your goals and plans pertaining to your purpose and destiny will be for the next 6 months. (Don't overwhelm yourself by writing a long list.)

   _____
   _____
   _____
   _____

Conclusion

Imagine you're planning an important trip and it happens entails a 20 mile mountain hike. The mere thought of the hike is very exciting and you allow yourself to get caught up in purchasing the gear so you can really "look" the part. As you're standing at the foot of the mountain and looking straight up at it you're trying to convince yourself to go ahead and make the climb. However, the longer you think about it the more you're convincing yourself why you shouldn't. You start to think about all kinds of things like falling, snake bites, being eaten by wild animals or just will I be able to make it to the top. Then you realize there's one good reason why you should move forward, press through and not get discouraged, that is; a sense of completion and conquering the difficult task. You finally make the decision to go ahead with the hike but not without making a deal with yourself; that you are not going to look down until you get to a certain point up the mountain.

As you're making the climb and you reach that point to look down, you discover that it really wasn't as bad as you thought it would be. And when you look at where you are as opposed to where you started you tell yourself "I've come too far to turn back now" and you proceed without any concern of any obstacles that will attempt to get in your way.

Sure, you're going to experience a few bumps and bruises along the way but once you reach the mountains peak you realize that it was well worth the trouble. Well don't you know that your success is similar to that mountain climb, yes it will seem difficult in the beginning when you look at all you will have to do to get there, and yes you will encounter some disappointments along the way, but once you reach that heightened level of success, you'll be glad that you did.

The "Sweet" Smell of Success

Many years ago my family and I took a trip to Hershey PA to visit the Hershey Amusement Park and tour the Chocolate Factory. If you've never visited the Hershey Factory it's really an awesome experience to watch how our favorite chocolates are birthed from a small cocoa bean to the savory tasting chocolate we purchase in our local stores. Before you even begin the tour you're met with a very potent chocolate aroma that was almost unbearable, but I was too excited about witnessing the end result so I continued walking through the long and at times boring and drawn out tour. But suddenly I am struck with an aroma that not only tells me the end is drawing near, but the product goal is almost complete. Finally, we reach the point where they showed us all the candies on the production line and boy what a site to behold. It's interesting to see how a small cocoa bean can produce a variety of chocolate candies in different shapes and sizes. Your success takes a similar journey. It may start out about the size of a cocoa bean, but once you work it to its fullest potential and add all the necessary ingredients, who knows what will manifest from that simple dream or vision. It's not about the size of your vision that matters most, but the effort that goes into realizing the potential of that vision.

We've finally reached the end of this era of your journey as it pertains to why you **were not** successful. But I am quite sure that after reading this book you're beginning to experience a more positive outlook than what you did prior to the starting this book. Did you notice that I said "were not" successful? I spoke in the past tense, because if you've made it this far, your success story is just beginning and you've finally made the decision that you "do" want to be successful. This book should be used as guide to get you started on your journey. You might have to start from scratch or at the last point where you stopped, always remember that it doesn't matter where you start, it only matters that you do.

Reinvent Yourself

It is said that "good things come to those who wait." But I believe that "great things come to those who will actually do something." Make life happen, don't allow life to make you. If you're not happy with where your life is headed right now, then it's about time that you do something different. Reinvent yourself! Reinventing yourself means taking what you already know how to do and repositioning yourself within it. You can start your own independent consulting firm after being downsized from a company you worked with for over 20 years or the former athlete who forms a training camp for youth after an injury forced an early retirement. Then there's the educator who lost their job but is now offering tutoring classes to academically challenged students. Whatever life tries to throw at you to knock you down, you need to know how to throw it right back remaining confident and strong in whom you were created to be. There is a world out there waiting for everything thing God has placed in you and if you don't make a quick decision to hear His voice and move at his notification, then without hesitation He will gladly pass it along to someone who is not afraid of what they see but they trust Who they know.

Hey, snap out of it! Put the book down and get moving, because I am looking forward to hearing you tell me all about your journey and how you **"Became Successful. . . Because You Wanted To Be."**

Success Summary Outline

CONGRATULATIONS! You have made it through to the final phase of your road to success. Hopefully you've acquired some valuable knowledge, insight and motivation that can be applied to the next steps in your journey. The only thing remaining for you to do now is to complete this Success Summary Outline. In this outline you will be asked to answer questions and/or provide additional details about your future plans. Its purpose is to really get you thinking about the future and maintaining a concentrated effort to follow through. Now let's get started!

Vision Summary

In 100 words or less write a complete detailed summary of your vision. Write it as if you were asked what it was you wanted to do and how you plan to get there. To help you out, think of it as a verbal proposal to a group of investors. Be sure that it describes the following;
- What – Provide details about your vision and your plans.
- When – Specify the exact date or time frame you expect to launch your business.
- Who – Describe your intended target market.
- Why – Purpose of the business and loan.
- How – Determine how you will repay any loans.

My Goal/Plan is

What's Your Passion?

Now that you've had an opportunity to share & express your vision, tell the investors why you're so passionate about this particular vision.

_____
_____
_____
_____
_____
_____
_____
_____

Staying Motivated

Briefly describe what methods you will use to keep yourself motivated. And then list at least three people, places or things that you've used or will continue to use to keep you motivated.

_____
_____
_____

1. _____
2. _____
3. _____

Education

List any tools or resources that you have begun to use or intend to use in order to increase your knowledge in your desired industry.

_____
_____
_____
_____
_____

Funding

1. I will need $_____.00 in capital in order to jump-start my business venture.

2. I have a total savings of $_____.00 and I am willing to invest _____% of that towards that initial capital investment.

3. If necessary, I am willing to offer _____% equity in my business to my investors.

4. I have decided to go with _____ as my primary lending source.

Final Summary

Within the next 90 days I will have successfully fulfilled at least one action item from each of the sections (Vision, Passion, Motivation, Education, Funding and Taking Action.)

Vision:
_____
_____

Passion:
_____
_____

Motivation:
_____
_____

Education:
_____
_____

Funding:
_____
_____

Taking Action:
_____
_____

Dear Future Success Story;

    I would like to personally thank you for allowing me to be a part of the first step in your journey to success. I'm sure that it wasn't easy but you managed to get this far so nothing should stop you from here on out. Success awaits you and when you're in direct alignment with the will of God everything that He desires for you to become *will* and *shall* come to pass. The best advice that I can offer you as we depart is; "don't be afraid of becoming successful." Take the challenges head on and toss them aside once you are done with them. You're a champion of success, so get up, hold your head up high and be proud of yourself.

Success, You've Got To See It, Believe It and Become It!

Yours Truly,

Suzan

Recommended Resources

Jack Canfield's Key to Living the Law of Attraction
Jack Canfield and D.D. Watkins

Reposition Yourself
Bishop T.D. Jakes

Who Moved My Cheese,
Spencer Johnson, M.D.

****

Booking Information

For more information on how to book Suzan' M. Stroud for your next event, seminar or conference:

Suzan' M. Stroud
PO Box 38521
Charlotte, NC 28278
Email: successful@carolina.rr.com

Made in the USA
Middletown, DE
10 October 2020